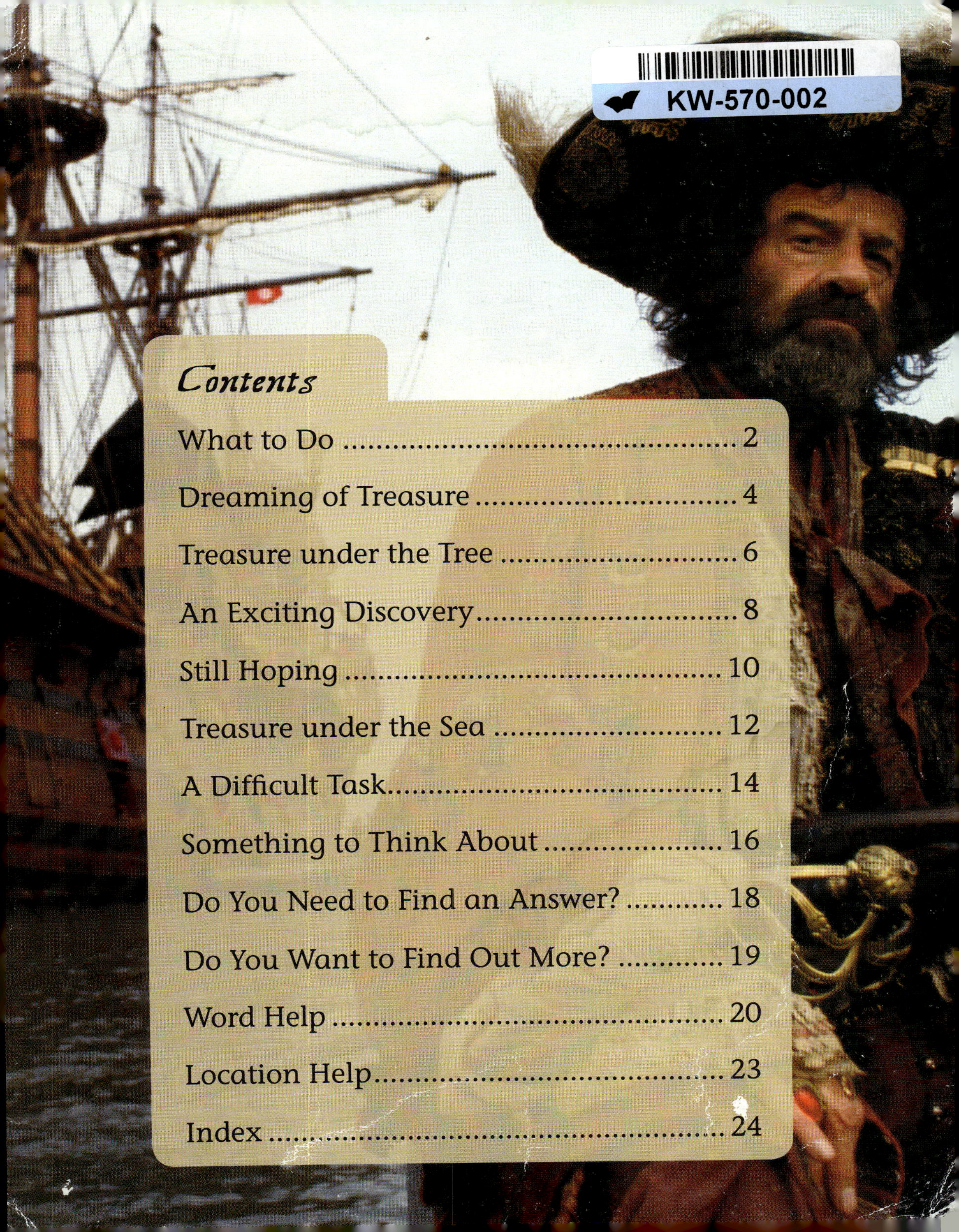

Contents

What to Do

Choose a face

Remember the colour you have chosen.

When you see your face on the page, you are the LEADER.

The LEADER reads the text in the speech bubbles.

There are extra words and questions to help you on the teacher's whiteboard. The LEADER reads these aloud.

When you see this stop sign, the LEADER reads it aloud.

You might need:

- to look at the WORD HELP on pages 20–22;
- to look at the LOCATION HELP on page 23;
- an atlas.

If you are the **LEADER**, follow these steps:

1 PREDICT

Think about what is on the page.

- Say to your group:

"I am looking at this page and I think it is going to be about…"

- Tell your group:

"Read the page to yourselves."

2 CLARIFY

Talk about words and their meaning.

- Say to your group:

"Are there any words you don't know?"

"Is there anything else on the page you didn't understand?"

- Talk about the words and their meanings with your group.
- Read the whiteboard.

- Ask your group to find the LET'S CHECK word in the WORD HELP on pages 20–22. Ask them to read the meaning of the word aloud.

3 ASK QUESTIONS

Talk about how to find out more.

- Say to your group:

"Who has a question about what we have read?"

- Question starters are: how…, why…, when…, where…, what…, who…
- Read the question on the whiteboard and talk about it with your group.

4 SUMMARISE

Think about who and what the story was mainly about.

When you get to pages 16–17, you can talk to a partner or write and draw on your own.

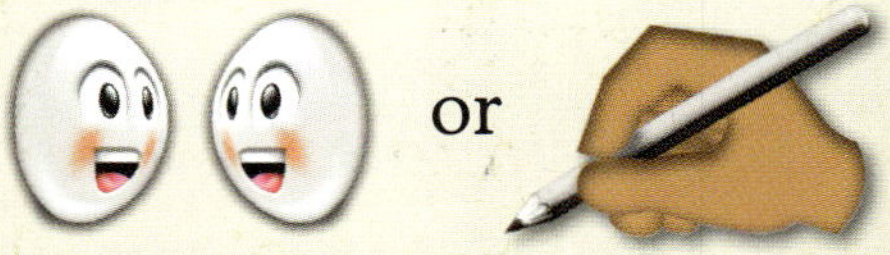

Dreaming of Treasure

I am looking at this page and I think it is going to be about... because...

Stories about pirates and buried treasure have been told for hundreds of years. Most are just **fiction**.

Captain Kidd, however, was thought to be a real pirate. He **attacked** a ship and stole its treasure. Some of the treasure he stole was found buried on an island. People thought there was still more treasure, but it has never been found.

Many people dream that they will find buried treasure. This dream has come true for some, but for others, not quite.

Are there any words you don't know?

Let's check: fiction

Who has a question about what we have read?

Why do you think that Captain Kidd might have buried the treasure?

Captain Kidd buries his treasure.

This page was mainly about
fact
fact

STOP
My predictions were right/wrong because . . .

Treasure under the Tree

I am looking at this page and I think it is going to be about... because...

Many years ago, so one story goes, a boy called Daniel went **exploring** on Oak Island.

Daniel saw marks on a tree that looked like rope marks. There was a **hollow** in the ground under the tree. Daniel thought of the stories he had heard about pirates and buried treasure. He thought these were a sign that there was treasure buried under the tree.

The next day, Daniel came back to the island with two friends and tools for digging.

Are there any words you don't know?

Let's check: hollow

Who has a question about what we have read?

Why do you think the rope marks might have been a sign of buried treasure?

This page was
mainly about
fact
fact
STOP
My predictions were right/wrong because . . .

An Exciting Discovery

I am looking at this page and I think it is going to be about… because…

Daniel and his friends began digging with **picks** and **shovels**. They hadn't dug far when they **discovered** some **slabs** of stone. This was an exciting discovery and the boys began to dig up the stones. Then, under the stones, they discovered logs. They could remove the logs, but to dig deeper, they knew they would need different tools.

It took nine years before Daniel and his friends returned to Oak Island. This time they had help to dig deeper.

Are there any words you don't know?

Let's check: slabs

Who has a question about what we have read?

Why do you think there might have been slabs of stone?

This page was mainly about
fact
fact

STOP
My predictions were right/wrong because . . .

Still Hoping

I am looking at this page and I think it is going to be about... because...

Many people began to help dig for the treasure. If treasure was found, they were **determined** to have a share in it.

Deep down they found a slab of stone with some **mysterious** writing on it. They were sure that the treasure was hidden under this stone. It was getting dark, so they had to leave. When they returned, the hole was filled with sea water.

The treasure was never found, but treasure hunters are still hoping that one day, it might be.

Are there any words you don't know?

Let's check: determined

Who has a question about what we have read?

Why do you think the men were sure that there was treasure under the stone?

'Forty feet below two million pounds are buried.' This is what some people think these strange symbols mean.

This page was mainly about

fact

fact

STOP

My predictions were right/wrong because . . .

Treasure under the Sea

I am looking at this page and I think it is going to be about... because...

The Whydah was a famous ship that was taken over by pirates. It sank a long time ago. On board the ship was gold, silver and other treasure.

About 300 years after it sank, the Whydah was found and so, too, were some of its treasures. Treasure hunters are still searching for more. They use a **magnetometer** and **digital** cameras to help them.

Treasure, worth millions of pounds, could be buried deep under the water.

Are there any words you don't know?

Let's check: magnetometer

Who has a question about what we have read?

How do you think digital cameras might help in the search for treasure?

Divers hold coins found on the wreck of the Whydah. The Whydah was a ship similar to the one pictured here.

A Difficult Task

I am looking at this page and I think it is going to be about… because…

People have always wanted to find real pirate treasure. But finding it is not easy. When a ship sinks, the heavy parts sink straight down. The treasure on board might be **scattered** a long way. It can be carried by the ocean **currents**.

This is why treasure hunters need a lot of information. They need to have good clues and the right tools.

When treasure is found, however, it can help to tell the stories of real pirates who lived long ago.

Are there any words you don't know?

Let's check: currents

Who has a question about what we have read?

What types of information do you think treasure hunters might need?

These divers are searching the seabed f
signs of treasure.

Something to Think About

or

Daniel and his friends shouldn't have told anyone about the treasure.

Yes No

If treasure hunters find any treasure, they should keep it for themselves.

Yes No

Treasure hunting is a waste of time and money.

Yes No

Think about what you have read about hunting for treasure. Read the words below. Do you agree? Talk about your ideas with a partner, or write them down.

Why?

Why?

Why?

Do You Need to Find an Answer?

You could go to . . .

Do You Want to Find Out More?

You could look in books or on the internet using these key words to help you:

Captain Kidd

Daniel McGinnis, treasure

Oak Island

pirates

pirate treasure

Whydah

Word Help

Dictionary

attacked	fought with or captured
currents	the steady flow of water or air in a direction
determined	having one's mind made up
digital	information that is changed into numbers and stored
discovered	found or saw something for the first time
exploring	looking carefully around a place
fiction	stories that are not real
hollow	a low place in the ground shaped like a bowl
magnetometer	a tool used to find hidden metal objects

mysterious	difficult to understand or explain
picks	pointy tools used to break rocks into smaller pieces
scattered	spread around
shovels	tools used for scooping and lifting things like sand
slabs	smooth flat pieces of rock or stone

Word Help

Thesaurus

buried	hidden, covered
searching	hunting
share	part, portion
sink	drop, fall
task	job, chore

Location Help

The Treasure Hunt Locations

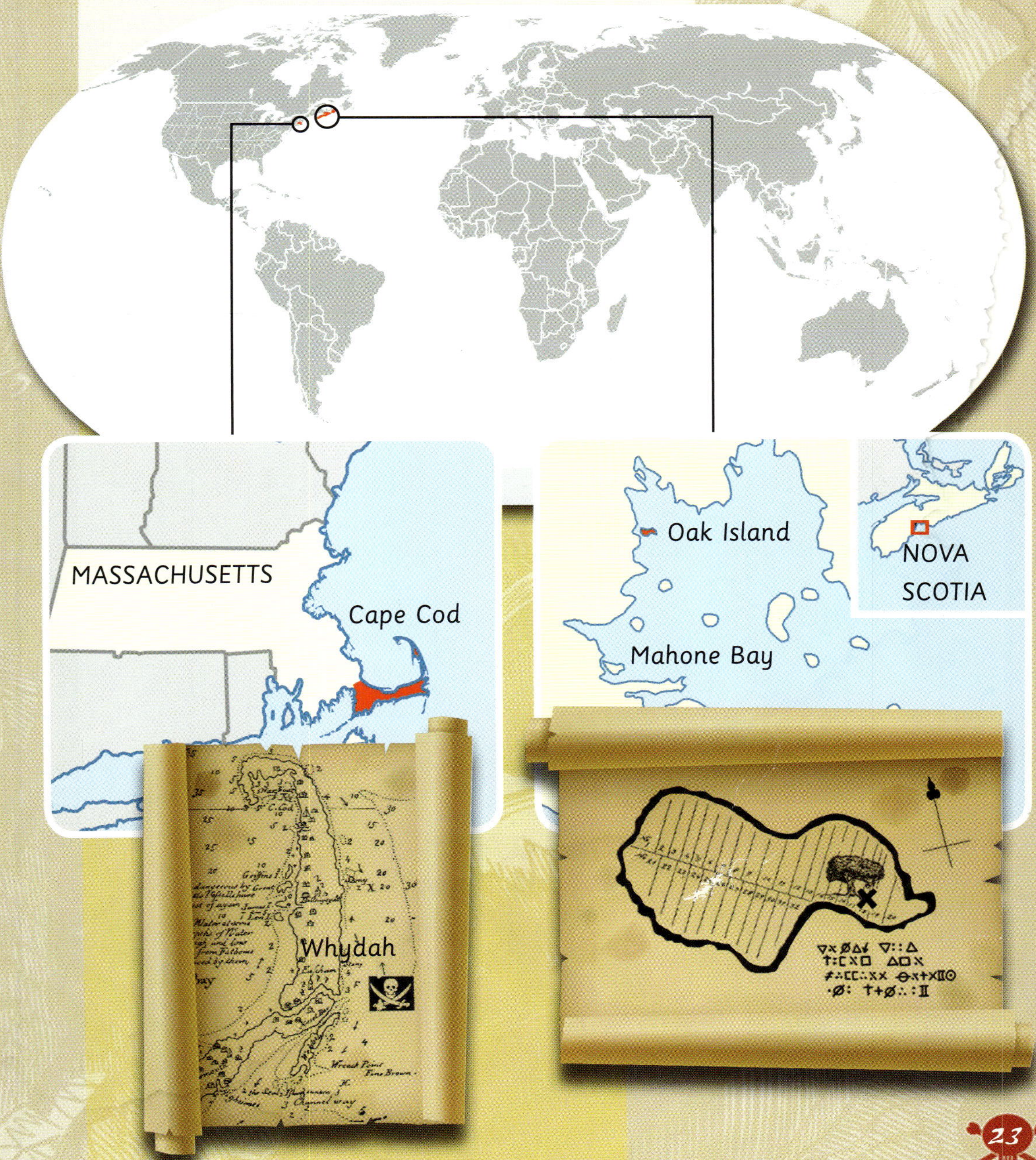

Index

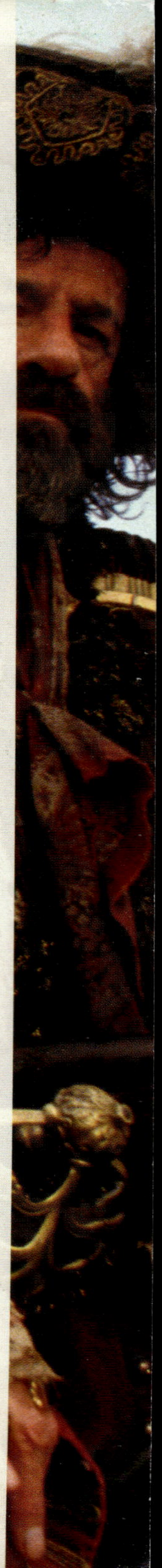